a hug from heaven

written by

Anna Whiston-Donaldson,
author of *Rare Bird*

illustrated by Andrea Alemanno

An Inch of Gray Press

A Hug From Heaven

For more information, please contact

info@annawhistondonaldson.com

ISBN: 979-8-9856081-1-3

Printed in the United States

For Jack, Margaret,
and Andrew

I went to heaven and that hurts your heart.
You don't like feeling that we're far apart.

You're glad I'm with God, in no sickness or pain.
But oh, how you wish you could hug me again.

Not in a decade or in 50 years.
You want me this minute, you want me right *here.*

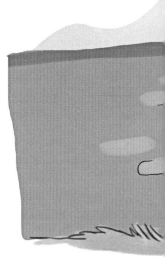

I'll tell you a secret that
may be a surprise.
When folks go to heaven,
their *love* never dies.

Nothing can steal love or
break it down,
not cancer or accidents.
No, love cannot drown.

My love for you and your
love for me
is still strong today and
always will be.

Sometimes you cry, and your tummy feels queasy.
Life seems unfair. Will it ever be easy?

Well, tears are okay. In fact, sometimes it's best
to let sadness flow out, to slow down and rest.

To say, "This is hard!
   I miss you so much!
I need your jokes and your
   gentle touch!"

Other times you may giggle
  and stifle a laugh
and think to yourself, "Is
  this the right path?"

Growing up happy,
  courageous, and kind
does not mean that you
  have left me behind.

I'm here to remind you what
some kids don't know:
I'll truly be with you
wherever you go.

Australia, Japan, New York, or Peru.
Wherever you are, I will be there too!

Cheering and clapping and saying "Well done!"
I want you to live life, learn, and have fun!

But how will you know that I'm by your side?
That I care and I see all the tears that you cry?

Well, God sees your sadness, your anger and pain,
the hot lonely tears that flow down like rain.

God knows that you need my hug and my kiss,
so He sends signs of love you won't want to miss.

It could be a rainbow high up in the sky,
a bird acting funny, or a huge butterfly.

A song that you hear at just the right time.
A lucky number, or finding a dime.

Peace on your shoulders,
a fluffy white cloud,
or rocks shaped like hearts
down on the ground.

A hug from heaven
fits like a glove.
Whatever it looks
like, the meaning
is *love.*

You may be wondering
what else you can do
to keep a close feeling
between me and you.

Sing on my birthday, look at photos in frames,
ask questions about me, and just say my name.

On trips and on holidays, look for a clue
to remind you I'm always, always with you.

Spend time outside. Tell me what's on your mind.
Write me letters and notes. I'm sure that you'll find

that thinking about me helps ease your pain
and none of your tears are ever in vain.

No matter what happens, I know you'll survive.
You'll live, you'll grow, and you'll learn how to thrive.

You'll never forget me, not ever, *nope!*
When you fill up your heart with love and with *hope.*

Remember, God loves both you and me.
There's nothing and no one that He doesn't see.

He made you, He loves you, He looks in your eyes
as He gently reminds you *our love never dies.*

This book is in memory of:

_____

I can use these pages to write
or draw how I feel in my grief

About the Author

Anna Whiston-Donaldson is the author of the New York Times bestseller Rare Bird: A Memoir of Loss and Love, which was selected as a Publishers Weekly Best Book of 2014. Anna's writing, public speaking, and teaching explores themes of grief, resilience, community, and faith. Connect with Anna at annawhistondonaldson.com.

Made in United States
North Haven, CT
12 September 2023

41460969R00020